Cave Dwellers

Contents

Inside a Cave 2

At the Front of the Cave 8

In the Twilight Zone 12

Into the Darkness 20

Other Cave Users 26

Index 32

Written by Sally Cole

Inside a Cave

Nearly all caves are dark, damp, and cool, because sunlight does not reach very far inside.

You would not think that these dark, damp places would be appealing. But there are some animals that seek shelter inside caves, and other animals that live in caves for most of their lives.

Plants, fungi, and algae, as well as animals, can also be found living in different parts of caves.

There are three parts to a cave – a sunlit area near the entrance, a twilight zone in the middle, and a dark area where no sunlight ever reaches at the back of the cave.

Cross-Section of a Cave

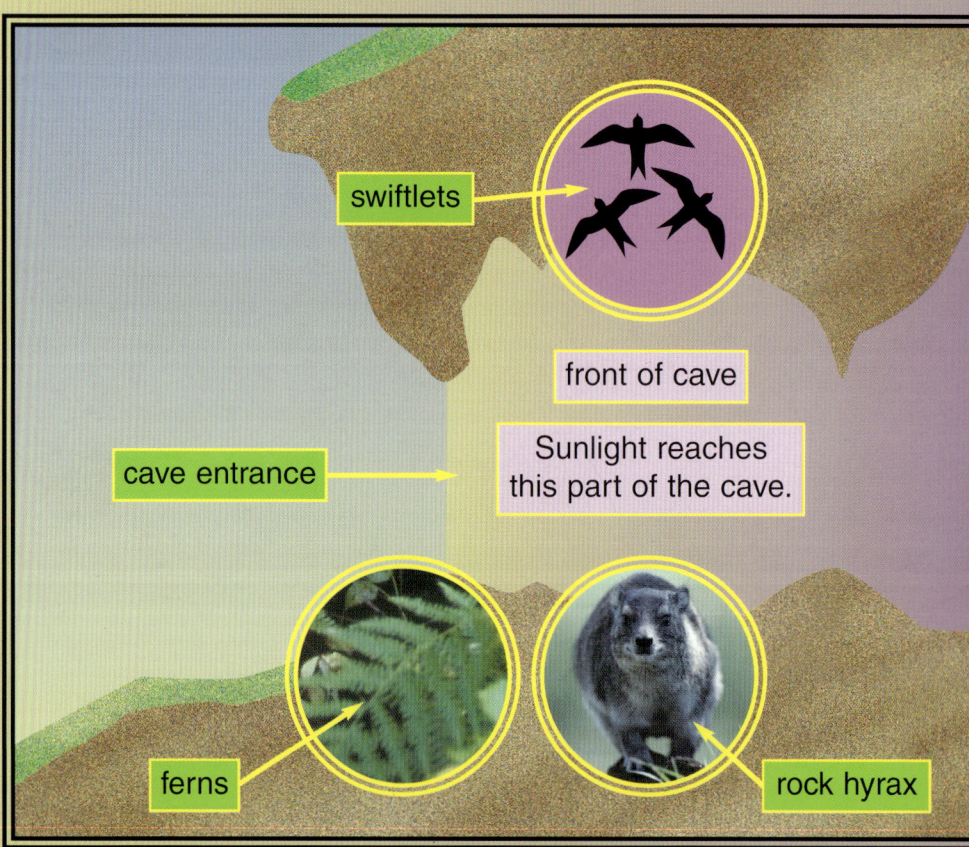

Plants like ferns live near the entrance where there is some light. Some fungi, like mushrooms, and some algae do not need sunlight to survive, so they live in the dark part of caves.

Animals looking for shelter may come to the sunlit part of the cave, and birds may be found nesting there.

middle of cave

back of cave

Animals spend time in caves for different reasons. Some animals, like bats, spend only the daylight hours sleeping in caves. Other animals use caves as a place to hide, while still others live their entire lives in caves.

Cross-Section of a Cave

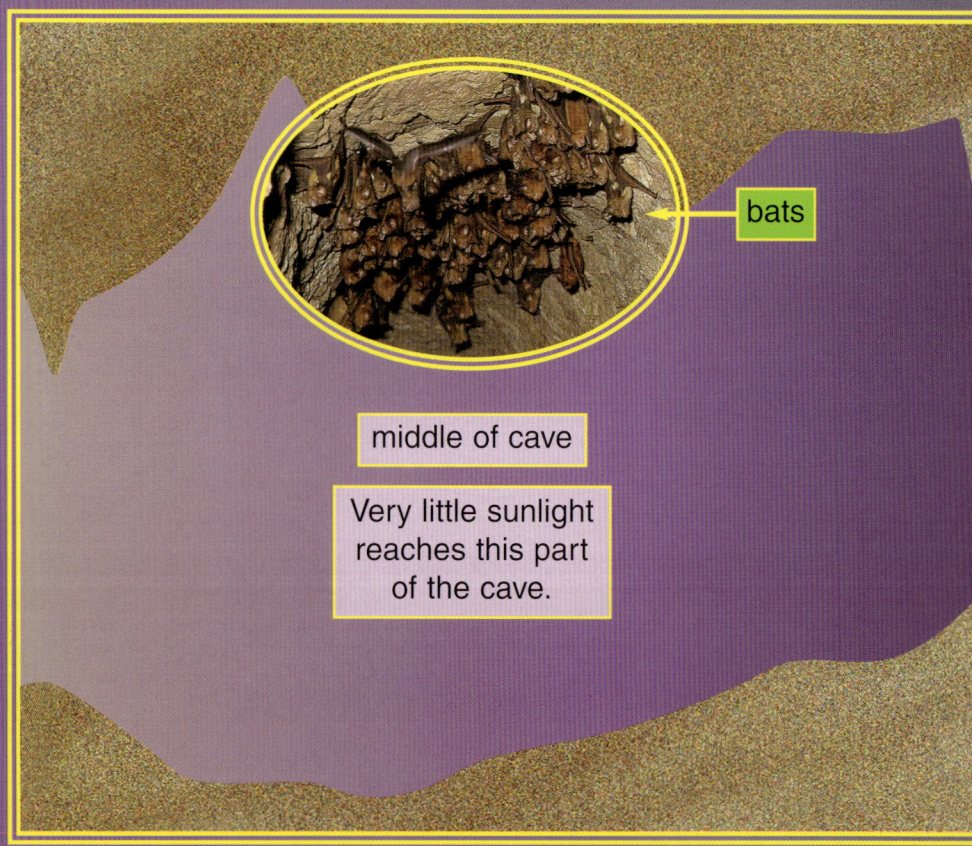

bats

middle of cave

Very little sunlight reaches this part of the cave.

Some of the animals that live in the dark at the back of caves are pale, white, or transparent. Some animals in this part of the cave are blind. They do not need to see because there is no sunlight and they spend all of their lives in darkness. When animals can't see, their other senses, such as touch and hearing, are often more developed.

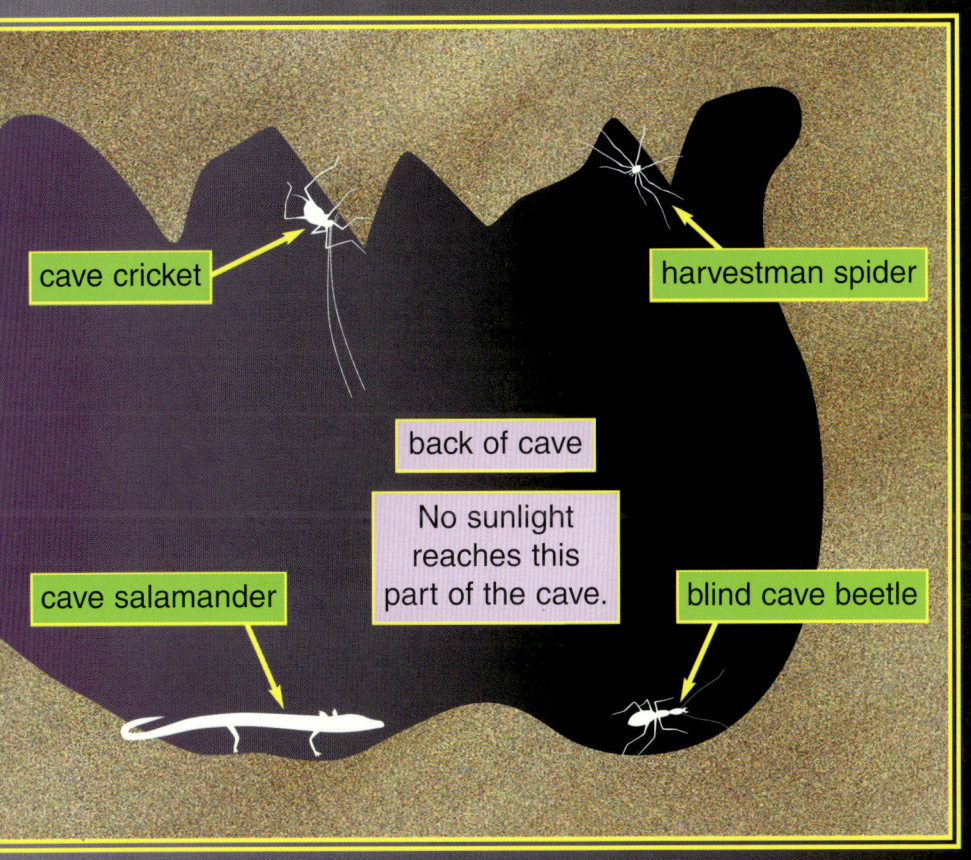

At the Front of the Cave

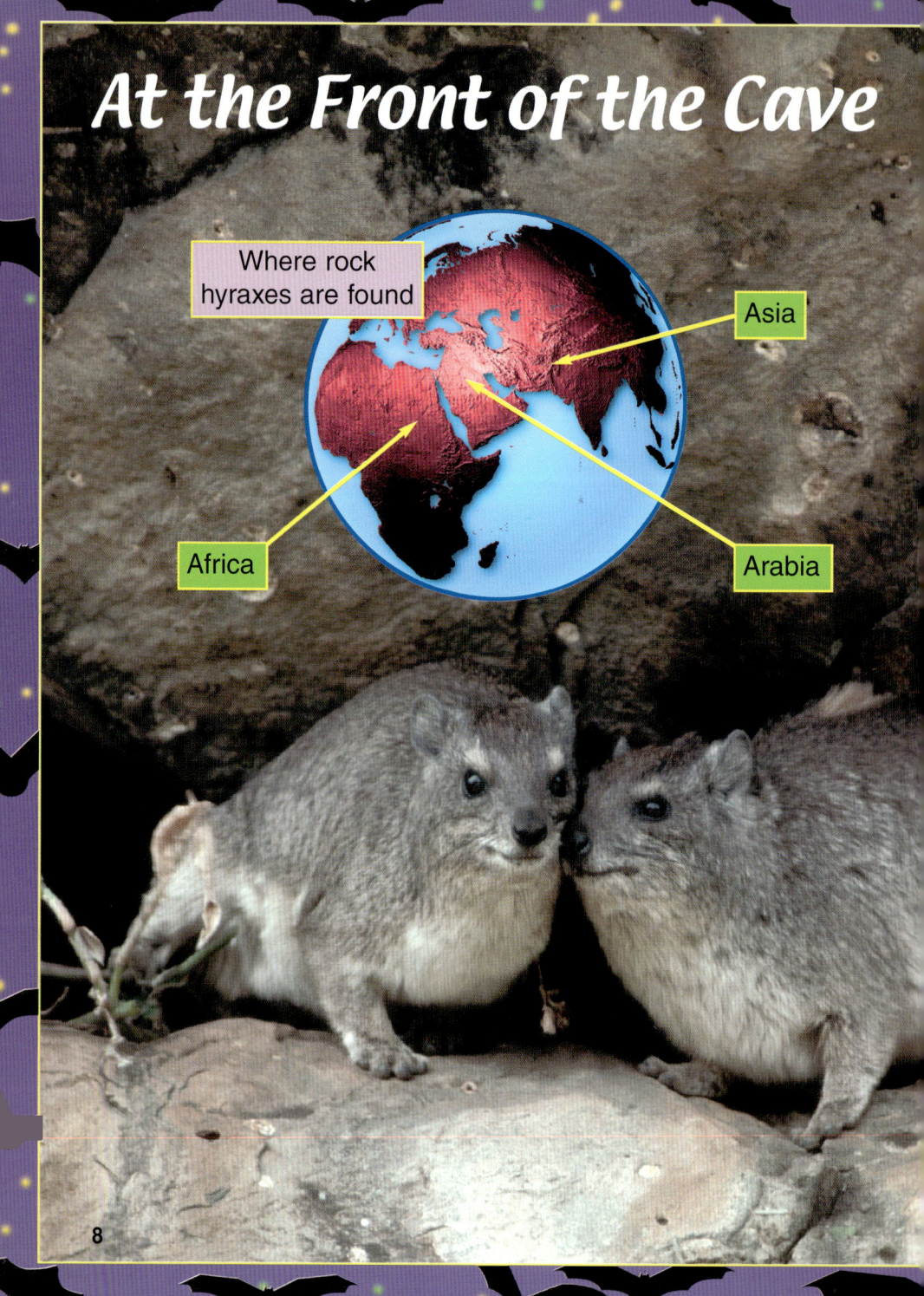

Where rock hyraxes are found

Asia

Africa

Arabia

Rock Hyraxes

Just inside the entrance of the cave, animals seek shelter from enemies and the weather. The rock hyraxes of Africa, Asia, and Arabia use caves as places to hide.

Hyraxes are mammals that look like big furry guinea pigs. Hyraxes are defenceless animals and survival depends on safe shelter.

During the day, families of hyraxes search for food. They eat mainly plants and berries. Rock hyraxes spend a lot of time lying in the sun.

The enemies of hyraxes are pythons, eagles, and big cats. When danger comes near, hyraxes will dash into caves for safety.

Size of Rock Hyrax

guinea pig   rock hyrax

Swiftlets

In some Malaysian caves, such as the Niah caves, in Sarawak, thousands of birds called swiftlets gather. They build their nests on the roofs of caves. These cup-shaped nests are made from the swiftlets' saliva. The saliva looks like spaghetti when it is fresh, but it hardens when it is exposed to the air.

Where swiftlets are found

Sarawak, Malaysia

Swiftlet in cup-shaped nest

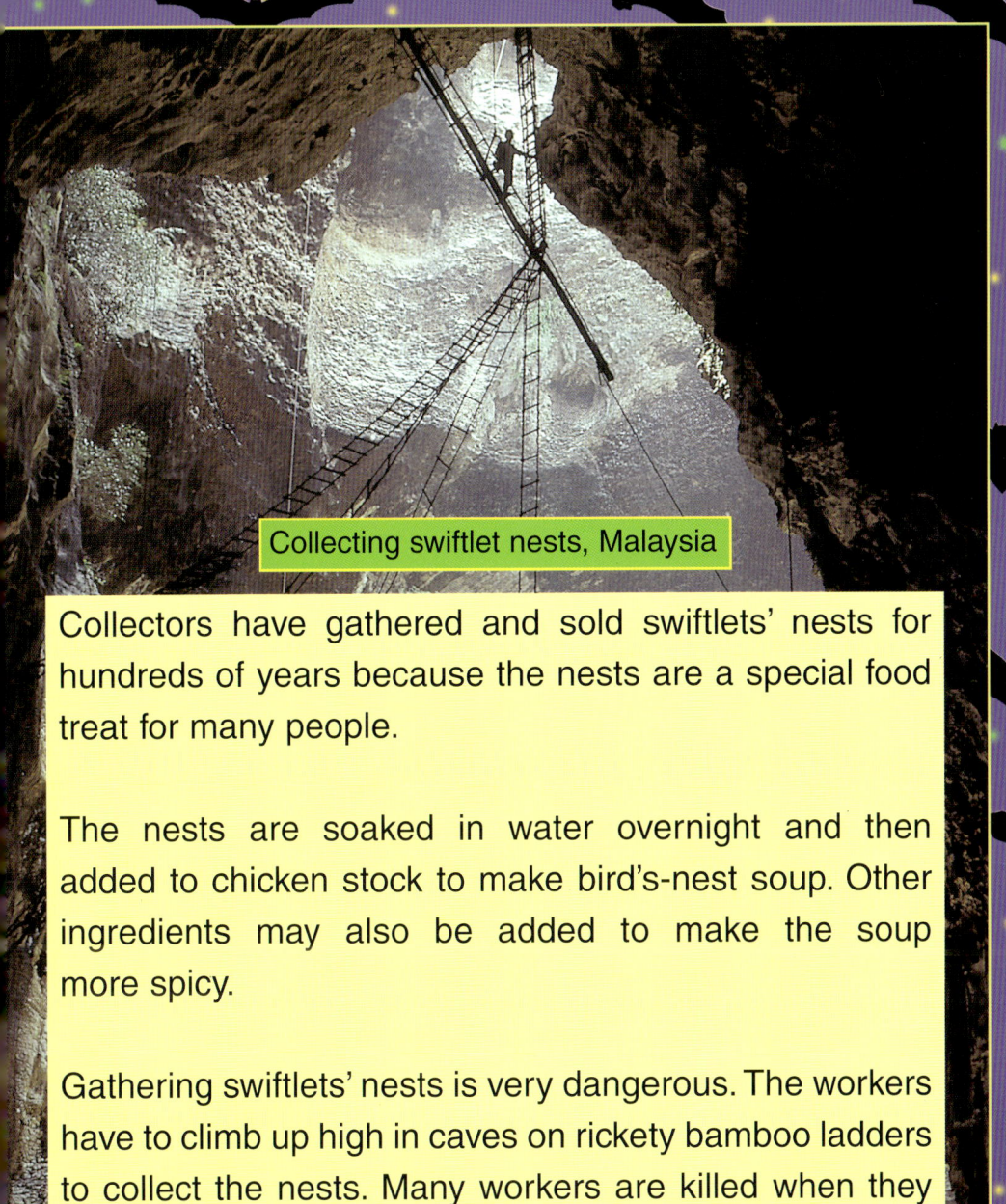

Collecting swiftlet nests, Malaysia

Collectors have gathered and sold swiftlets' nests for hundreds of years because the nests are a special food treat for many people.

The nests are soaked in water overnight and then added to chicken stock to make bird's-nest soup. Other ingredients may also be added to make the soup more spicy.

Gathering swiftlets' nests is very dangerous. The workers have to climb up high in caves on rickety bamboo ladders to collect the nests. Many workers are killed when they fall from the ladders.

In the Twilight Zone

Guacharo Birds

The caves of Venezuela, in South America, are where guacharo birds live. These birds are about the size of chickens. They are also known as oilbirds. The oil from the birds' bodies is used by the Indians of northern South America for cooking. They also burn the oil in their lamps for light.

Guacharo birds stay in their caves all day. At night they leave the cave to feed, mostly on fruit from the forest.

When guacharo birds fly outside at night, their large, round, owl-like eyes help them to find food.

When they fly inside caves, guacharo birds find their way in the dark using sound waves. They make high, screeching sounds that bounce off cave walls. The birds have special sensors that pick up sound waves and tell them how near or far the wall is. This prevents the guacharo bird from crashing into cave walls.

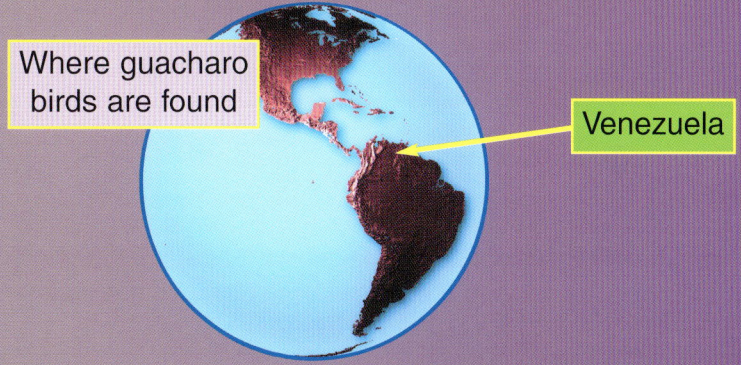

Where guacharo birds are found

Venezuela

Guacharo birds in a cave

Bats

Bats are the only mammals that can fly. They live in caves, often in huge groups called colonies. Bats have wings of fine skin that look as though they are made of leather. These wings are joined to bats' bodies from their necks to their back legs. The back feet, toes, and sharp curved claws of bats are very strong. They use them to hold on to the cave roof while they sleep hanging upside down.

Bats sleep all day, then as night falls they leave the cave in search of food. Some bats live on insects, while others eat fruit.

Bats use strong back feet, toes, and sharp curved claws to hang from cave roofs.

Bats find their way around dark caves in much the same way as guacharo birds. They make very high-pitched squeaks. The squeaks are so high-pitched that people cannot hear them. When these sound waves hit something, they bounce back as an echo. The bats have sensors that pick up the echo. The time it takes the echo to reach the bat tells it how far away an object is.

Bats use sound waves to find their way around dark caves.

The New Zealand Glowworm

The Waitomo Caves, in New Zealand, are the home of the New Zealand glowworm. These glowworms are really the larvae stage of the fungus gnat. They are similar to glowworms found in Tasmania and south-eastern Australia. But they are not the same as the American glowworm which is the larvae stage of a type of beetle.

New Zealand glowworms need a special habitat to survive, and the caves at Waitomo and other New Zealand locations provide such a habitat. Glowworms, first needs are humidity to stop them drying out and darkness to allow them to show their light. Their other needs revolve around food.

Glowworms need an adequate food supply and a hanging surface which allows them to send down feeding lines to catch their food. They also need the atmosphere to be still so that these feeding lines do not become tangled.

There are four stages to a glowworm's life-eggs, larva, pupa and adult. The whole cycle takes about 11 months. Adult glowworms live for only a few days and in that time they mate and the female lays eggs. She lays up to 120 eggs in clusters of 30-40 on the cave walls and ceiling.

As soon as the larvae hatch, they emit light. This light is more efficient than the average light bulb because 90 percent of the power that glowworms generate is light.

Where New Zealand glowworms are found

New Zealand, location of the Waitomo Caves

Straight after hatching, glowworms make silk nests which they stick to the roofs of caves. From each nest they send down as many as 70 feeding lines. These long threads are lined with tiny, sticky pearls of mucus. Glowworms feed mainly on small insects, called midges, that breed in the water and mud banks beneath them. In the darkness, midges are attracted by the glowworms' light. They fly up and become caught in the sticky feeding lines. The glowworm then moves from the nest to the thread where the midges are stuck. It hauls up the thread and eats the midges. The hungrier glowworms are, the more light they emit to attract their prey.

midge

Glowworm and silk feeding lines

Glowworms remain as larvae for about 9 months, growing from 0.1 inches (3 mm) to over 1 inch (25 mm) long. This is the only stage when glowworms feed. They need an abundant food supply at this stage so that they can store food to survive the pupa and adult stage.

At the pupa stage, glowworms shrink, become opaque, and hang vertically from a long thread. The pupa stage lasts about 12 days. Before an adult female emerges from the pupa stage, her light becomes more brilliant, probably to attract a male.

Many people visit the glowworm caves at Waitomo to see the amazing sights. The ceilings of the caves are lit up by thousands of glowworms glowing in the darkness.

People viewing the glowworms at the Waitomo Caves.

Into the Darkness

At the back of the cave, the light never shines.

White fungus grows on the floor of some caves. This fungus is food for many of the insects which live in the darkest part of the cave.

Many insects feed on white fungus on the cave floor.

Cave Crickets

Cave crickets have grown so used to life in the dark that they cannot survive outside the cave. In some cases their antennae grow up to four times as long as their bodies. They use their antennae to feel their way around the dark caves.

The antennae of cave crickets can be four times as long as their bodies.

Salamanders

In some caves in Texas, Georgia, and the Appalachian Mountains, in the United States, you can find many salamanders living in the darkest parts of the caves. These salamanders are very pale, with long, thin legs and a blunt, rounded snout. Some have no eyes, and so their bodies are very sensitive to anything that comes near them. They usually lay eggs under rocks in the water. Once hatched, they can live up to 25 years.

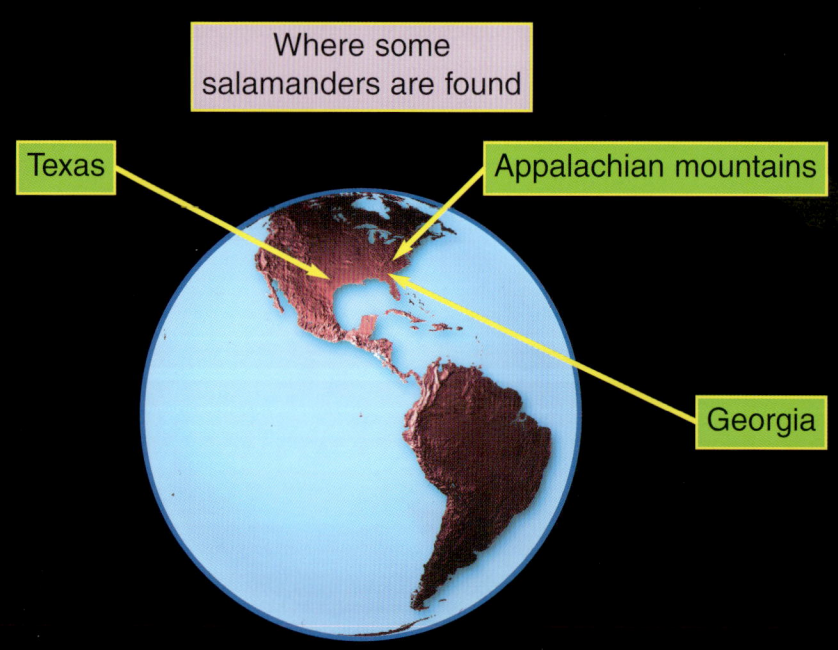

Where some salamanders are found

But, the first salamander found living in a cave was not in the United States. It was found over 300 years ago in Yugoslavia, in Europe. Because the villagers living in the area had never seen anything like a salamander before, they said it looked like a mythical dragon.

Texas blind salamander

On the floor at the back of many caves there are spiders, crickets, beetles, and lots of other creeping, swimming, jumping critters.

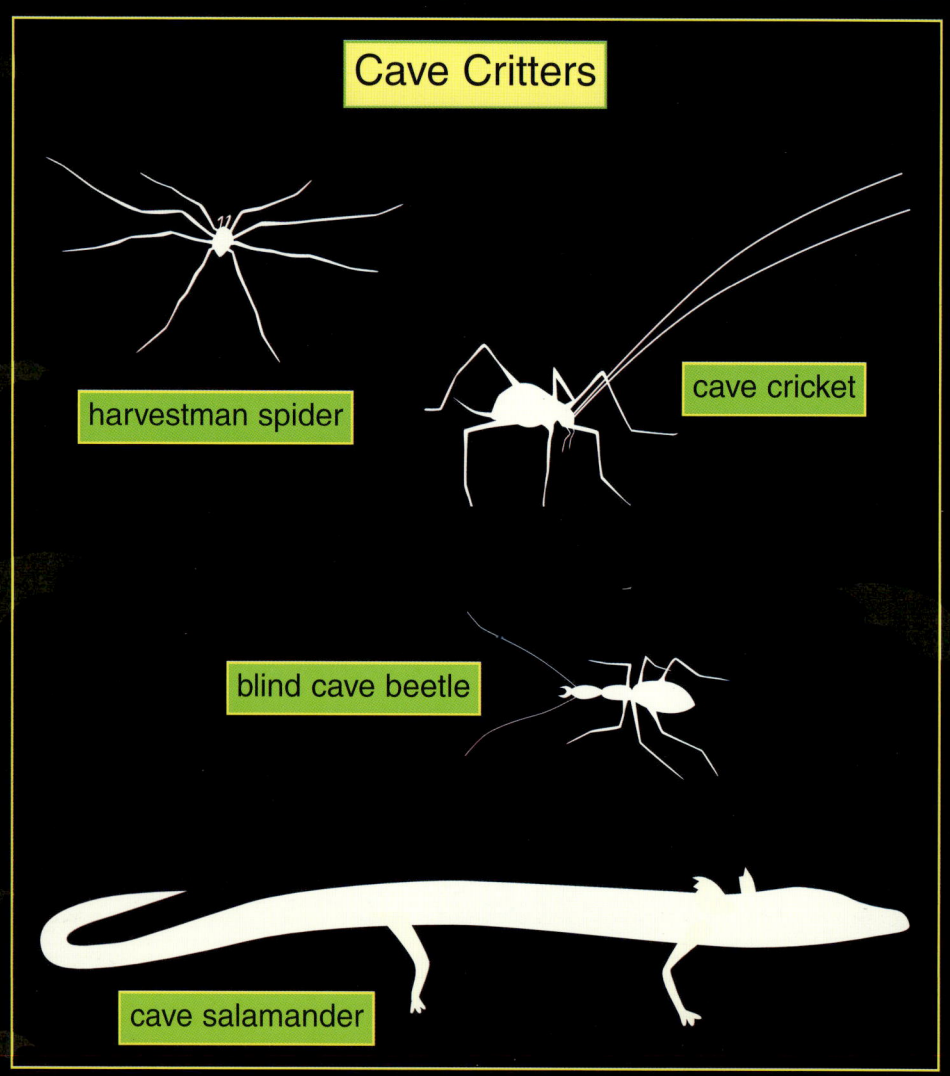

Cave Critters

harvestman spider

cave cricket

blind cave beetle

cave salamander

Scientists are still finding new animals living in caves around the world. In 1981, a blind, transparent creature was found in an underwater cave on Grand Bahama Island. It looked like a worm with many legs. This animal turned out to be a direct descendant of animals that swam in the tropical oceans millions of years ago.

Grand Bahama Island

Other Cave Users

Bears

Archeologists, people who study ancient civilizations and cultures by examining remains and artifacts, have found evidence that bears have been using caves for thousands of years.

In the Chavet Cave, in France, archeologists have found bear footprints, traces of their claws and fur, and scratchings on the walls. Today, we know that some bears hibernate in caves. These hibernating bears spend their winters sleeping inside a cave. They store enough food as fat in their bodies to last them until spring.

Black bear and cub in a cave

Sometimes the female bears give birth to their cubs in the caves. In the spring the cubs stay in the cave for safety while their mother goes hunting. Once the cubs are big enough to take care of themselves, they will leave the cave.

Bears that Hibernate in Caves	Bears that Do Not Hibernate in Caves
Moon bears American black bears	Brown bears Polar bears Sun bears Sloth bears Spectacled bears Giant pandas

Human Cave Dwellers

Through the centuries caves have been homes or shelters for different people around the world. Today some people still use caves as their homes.

Archeologists have found things in caves to show that humans were using caves thousands of years ago. Hand prints and human-like figures printed or etched on cave walls, as well as human-like skulls and skeletons, suggest that these early humans looked similar to humans today.

Hands painted on a cave wall, Borneo, Indonesia

Studies of human and animal remains along with art on cave walls suggest to archeologists ways that early humans may have used caves.

Archeologists think that people usually lived near the entrance to caves in the winter. The entrance would have provided shelter from the weather. It also provided a place where people could light fires for warmth and to cook food. If people had lit fires further inside caves there would have been nowhere for the smoke to escape.

Native American wall painting

It seems likely that the darkest, back part of caves may have been used for ceremonies and rituals. It was in this part of caves that early humans painted, etched, or printed pictures. As it is dark in the back of caves, people who made cave pictures would have had to use torches to provide light. Archeologists think that animal fat was used for torch fuel.

Lascaux cave paintings

Cave paintings also provide insights into the lives of these early humans. People are often shown hunting, running, dancing, and throwing spears. The number of times that animals appear on cave walls also suggests that these were important in the lives of early human cave dwellers. It is possible that early people used animals to provide food and clothing, in much the same way as people do today.

Index

antennae 21

bird's-nest soup 11

cave paintings 31

colonies 14

echo 15

ferns 4, 5

fruit 12, 14

insects 14, 20

nests 10, 11

shelter 5, 9

sunlight 3, 4, 5